YOUR KNOWLEDGE HAS VALUE

- We will publish your bachelor's and master's thesis, essays and papers

- Your own eBook and book - sold worldwide in all relevant shops

- Earn money with each sale

Upload your text at www.GRIN.com and publish for free

Oliver Baumgartner

Basel 3 capital requirements - overview and critical evaluation

GRIN Verlag

Bibliografische Information der Deutschen Nationalbibliothek:

Die Deutsche Bibliothek verzeichnet diese Publikation in der Deutschen National-
bibliografie; detaillierte bibliografische Daten sind im Internet über http://dnb.d-
nb.de/ abrufbar.

Imprint:

Copyright © 2012 GRIN Verlag GmbH
Druck und Bindung: Books on Demand GmbH, Norderstedt Germany
ISBN: 978-3-656-36902-8

This book at GRIN:

http://www.grin.com/en/e-book/209183/basel-3-capital-requirements-overview-
and-critical-evaluation

GRIN - Your knowledge has value

Der GRIN Verlag publiziert seit 1998 wissenschaftliche Arbeiten von Studenten, Hochschullehrern und anderen Akademikern als eBook und gedrucktes Buch. Die Verlagswebsite www.grin.com ist die ideale Plattform zur Veröffentlichung von Hausarbeiten, Abschlussarbeiten, wissenschaftlichen Aufsätzen, Dissertationen und Fachbüchern.

Visit us on the internet:

http://www.grin.com/

http://www.facebook.com/grincom

http://www.twitter.com/grin_com

Basel 3: capital requirements

WS 2012/2013

Innsbruck University School of Management

Baumgartner Oliver

I.   Table of content

II. Table of figures

III. List of abbreviations

ABS – Asset Backed Security

BCBS – Basel Committee of Banking Supervision

CDO – Collateralized Debt Obligation

CDS – Credit Default Swap

GDP – Gross Domestic Product

IRB – Internal Rating Based

NINJA – No Income, No Asset, No Job

OECD – Organization for Economic Co-operation and Development

OTC – Over The Counter

ROE – Return On Equity

RWAs – Risk weighted Assets

SME – Small and Middle-sized Entrepreneurs

SPV – Special Purpose Vehicle

1. Introduction

The implementation of capital requirements in the banking sector is done by the Basel Committee of Banking Supervision. Historically, these requirements got upgraded step-by-step to prevent high risk in this sector. Although, this was the aim of all Basel accords, the last financial crisis has shown us the shortcomings that they still have.

This paper is divided in to three main parts where each has some subdivisions:

Firstly, one will get a basic overview about the history of the whole Basel Accord. The implementation of the new Basel III capital requirements was not that easy and was not a work of only a few days. It started quite early in the mid-70s with the foundation of the Basel Committee. During the years the Basel accord was enhanced a lot of times until the latest version was presented in 2010.

Secondly, there is an in-depth explanation of the whole capital requirements under Basel III. One will see the changes between the requirements under Basel II and III. Especially the division of Tier 1 and 2 capital has changed dramatically. Additionally, there is an exact explanation of different types of money sources which can be used as Tier 1 or 2 capital. Essential new types of capital are the two Buffers that are going to be implemented under Basel III – Countercyclical and Conversation Buffer.

Thirdly, there are also some discussions going on with Basel III. Although, the higher capital requirements make the banking sector safer, there are a few shortcomings for the whole economy. One will see three main shortcomings, which are often discussed by researchers. Additionally, one finds a part where I explain my personal critics about the new Basel III capital requirements.

Finally, at the end of this paper one will get a short conclusion about the content of the whole paper. After reading all parts one should be able to understand the system of Basel, including all its Pros and Cons.

2. Historical Development

Generally, the banking regulations of Basel I, II and III are made by the Basel Committee on Banking Supervision (BCBS). This Committee was founded in 1974 by the G-10 with the intention to provide a forum of discussion, make the coordination between national supervisors easier and to improve the overall supervisory standards that should lead to a better financial stabilization. Meanwhile it consists of more states and has its' headquarter in Basel. The decisions which are made in the Basel Committee have no legal status and are therefore not obligatory under international law. In its early stages, the aim was that all banks which are internationally active have to implement some rules which are made by the Basel Committee (Basel I, II and III). Meanwhile, these rules should be implemented by all banks around the world to guarantee a stable financial environment. One reason behind this is that the increasing globalisation crosslinks the business of banks all around the world. Hence, the Basel Committee decided to implement the first Basel Accord which introduced the first capital requirements for the banking system. [1]

2.1. Basel I

To understand why the implementation of Basel I was necessary one has to understand how the business of a bank works. Basically, banks get money from their clients in form of deposits. This short term deposits can then be used to give loans to clients. Normally, these clients have to pay a higher interest rate on their long term loans in comparison with the interest rate they get from short term deposits. The difference between these interest rates is the main profit of a bank. Therefore, it is the main problem for a bank if clients cannot payback their loans or if the banks do not get enough deposits to maintain their loan business. Generally, such situations are not that harmful as long as a bank has enough equity to absorb its losses. The lower the amount of equity compared to its total assets is, the higher is the risk that the bank will face a liquidity problem. The liquidation of the German Herstatt bank was a major signal that showed how important it is to have enough equity, to maintain in the banking business. [2]

---

[1] BCBS
[2] King et. Al. (2011)

4

In an US study of Berger et. al. it is shown that the overall equity rate, as a percentage of total assets, has decreased sharply since 1840. Especially, one can see a very low rate beginning in the mid-70s. Figure 1 gives a detailed overview of the development of equity in the US banking business.

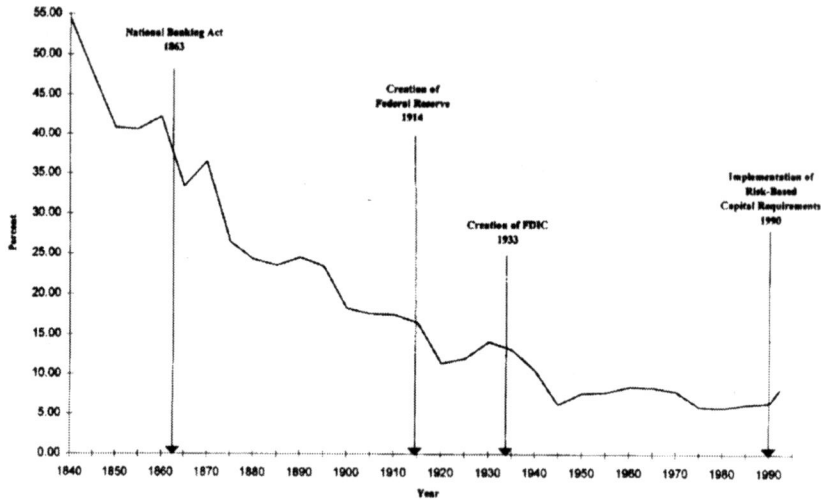

Figure 1: Total equity rates in US Commercial banks from 1840-1990 [3]

There was a decline in the equity ratio from 55 down to 5 percent. The BCBS argued that banks are not able to maintain their business during a crisis, when they only have such low equity ratios. Hence, they implemented Basel I in the year 1988. One of the goals of this rule was to get a higher stability in the banking system. Additionally, it was encouraged that all banks have the same minimum amount of equity to make it possible that there are no distortions of competition. Under Basel I there was also the first definition of Tier 1 and 2 capital, which is also used in the latest version of Basel Accords. Tier 1 and 2 capital are different forms of equity which are hold by a bank. By definition, a bank has to hold a minimum of 8 percent of its risk weighted Assets (RWAs) in form of equity under Basel I. For the calculation under the Basel I version from 1988 there was only credit risk which was taken into account. [4]

---

[3] Berger et. Al. (1995), p.402
[4] Basel I (1998)

The risk weights were defined very easily. There were four different risk weighting categories:

- 0 percent: cash, claims to OECD countries
- 20 percent: claims to OECD banks, public institutions
- 50 percent: loans which are secured by mortgage
- 100 percent: all other claims to corporate or private clients [5]

In the year 1996 the BCBS realized that there has to be an additional amount of equity, to absorb potential losses from trading business. Therefore, market risk was introduced in the calculation of RWAs. One important critic about Basel I is the bad definition of risk weighting factors. E.g. claims to different OECD countries got the same weight, regardless of which rating they got. Therefore, the risk in the banks business couldn't be covered by its equity in times of a crisis. Additionally, there was no clear definition about Tier 1 and Tier 2 capital. Due to these and other problems the BCBS introduced Basel II in the year 2004. [6]

2.2. Basel II

Like in Basel I the main goal with the implementation of Basel II was to strengthen equity ratios of banks. The BCBS encouraged this upgrade of the Basel accord due to some critical points under the first approach. E.g. the RWAs were used for clients with a different possibility of default. Therefore, banks had the incentive to give more loans to customers which were riskier, because they could charge a higher interest rate. Some definitions under the Basel I accord were not properly explained. Banks used this as an advantage to interpret it like they want it. Additionally, some things like operational risk or a supervisory review process were not defined. Hence, it was quite easy to manipulate the amount of RWAs. As a result these problems led to lower equity rate than it should be. [7]

---

[5] Basel I (1998), p.17-18
[6] King et. Al. (2011)
[7] Balin (2008)

Due to all these and some more facts the document of Basel II was finished in the year 2004. The plan was that it should be implemented in the year 2006 by all banks. The new Basel II accord was built on three main pillars: (1) minimum capital requirement (2) Supervisory Review Process and (3) Market discipline. Because this paper mainly deals with the capital requirements of Basel III, I will only explain briefly pillar 1 of Basel II. The amount of 8 percent of RWAs as equity capital was kept constant under the new Basel accord. But now also operational risk was introduced in the calculations. E.g. operational risks can be mistakes that are caused by humans in the normal business process. [8]

Especially, the calculation of credit risk was improved under Basel II. Banks had the possibility to calculate their credit risk with 3 different methods: standardized-, internal rating based (IRB) foundation- and IRB advanced approach. When a bank decided to use the standardized approach it had to get some external ratings to determine single risk weights. The better the external rating, the lower the probability of default and therefore, the lower the equity that has to be hold. The risk weights which are used are between 0 and 150 percent. When a bank wanted to calculate the risk weights on their own they can use the IRB approach, which can be subdivided into foundation and advanced IRB. When a bank uses the foundation approach it had to estimate only the probability of default. The advanced IRB approach needed additionally the Loss given that a default occurs, maturity of the Asset and the exposure at default. [8]

Under Basel II there is a clear definition how the distribution of the 8 percent RWAs should look like. On the one side it consists of Tier 1 capital that *"includes only permanent shareholders' equity"* [9] Examples are therefore common stock, some preferred shares with perpetual features and capital reserves. Furthermore the 8 percent of RWAs consists of Tier 2 capital. By definition, Tier 2 capital consists of undisclosed reserves, loan loss reserves and subordinated debt. Additionally, there are some limits on the amounts of Tier 1 and 2 capital. Tier 2 capital is limited to a maximum of 100 percent of Tier 1 capital. Therefore, the 8 percent equity was built of 4 percent Tier 1 and 4 percent Tier 2 capital, like it is shown in Figure 2. [8]

Although all these updates were implemented, the last financial crisis has shown that also Basel II had still some weaknesses.

---

[8] Basel II (2006)
[9] Basel II (2006), p.245

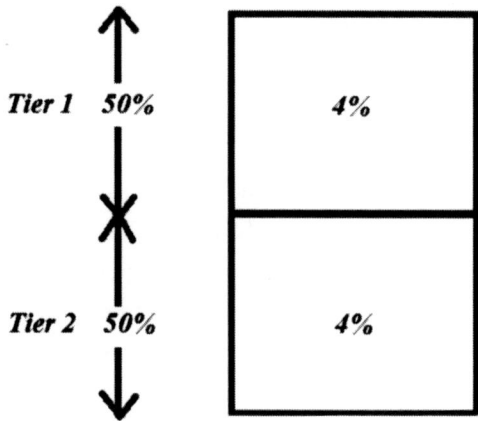

Tier 1   50%   4%

Tier 2   50%   4%

Figure 2: Distribution of minimum capital requirement under Basel II [10]

During the financial crisis, banks constructed financial products like Asset backed securities (ABS) or collateralized debt obligations (CDO). These products bundled loans and made it able to sell them to other banks. Therefore, banks were able to shift the risk away and also decrease the RWAs. Hence, they had not to hold that much equity. Sometimes banks were able to hold only an equity ratio of about 1 percent according to these new financial products. Additionally, the risk weights for Assets in the trading book were relatively low in comparison to Assets in the banking book. This fact strengthened the problem which came with ABSs and CDOs. Another problem was the new calculation method of credit risk. The rating agencies were unable to calculate adequate ratings for ABSs and CDOs. Therefore, they had a better rating compared with their risk involved. Additionally, the possibility that banks could calculate all estimates on their own under the IRB approach led to too low risk weights. All these reasons ended in a too low amount of equity in almost every bank. However, the new Basel 3 capital requirements should improve all the shortcomings that the previous accord had. [11]

---

[10] own creation; information out of Basel (2006)
[11] King et. Al. (2011)

3. Basel III

After the financial crisis with its peak in 2007, many countries claimed for stricter rules in the banking regulation system. Therefore, the BCBS discussed the shortcomings during the financial crisis and presented the new Basel 3 accord at the end of 2010. The main changes include that the capital ratio, including all possible buffers, increased to a level of 13 percent of its RWAs. Another goal is to define each part of this capital in more detail as it was done in previous accords. However, the BCBS thought there should not be a method which only looks at RWAs. Hence, there is a leverage ratio implemented which compares only Tier 1 capital with its total exposure. The new liquidity requirements are not explained in this paper. [12]

3.1. 8% Total and 13% Potential Capital Ratio

Due to the fact that banks had not enough equity during the financial crisis to cover their losses, the BCBS decided to increase the Total Capital Ratio. However, they added some new parts in this ratio like the conservation and countercyclical buffers. To get a basic knowledge about all the consisting facts which influence this ratio, one has to look at its setup. Hence, figure 3 provides an overview of the 8 percent Total Capital and the 13 percent potential Capital Ratio. Generally, one can see that there are more subdivisions of capital under Basel III. The Total Capital Ratio consists of three parts: 4.5% Common Equity Tier 1, 2% Additional Tier 1 and 2% Tier 2 Capital. Under Basel II the distribution was 50/50 between Tier 1 and 2 capital. Under the new Basel II accord, banks have to hold at least 75 percent in form of Tier 1 capital if we do not take the buffers into account. A smaller percentage is needed as Tier 2 capital. However, the BCBS decided to introduce some buffers to make the equity situation in banks more stable. Basically, these are the Conversation and Countercyclical Buffer. The Conversation Buffer consists of 2.5% Common Equity Tier 1 and the Countercyicilical Buffer of 0-2.5% Tier 1 Capital. Therefore, the overall distribution between Tier 1 and 2 Capital under Basel III is 85 to 15 percent. The next chapters will explain every single part of the capital requirements in more detail. [13]

---

[12] King et. Al. (2011)
[13] Basel III (2011)

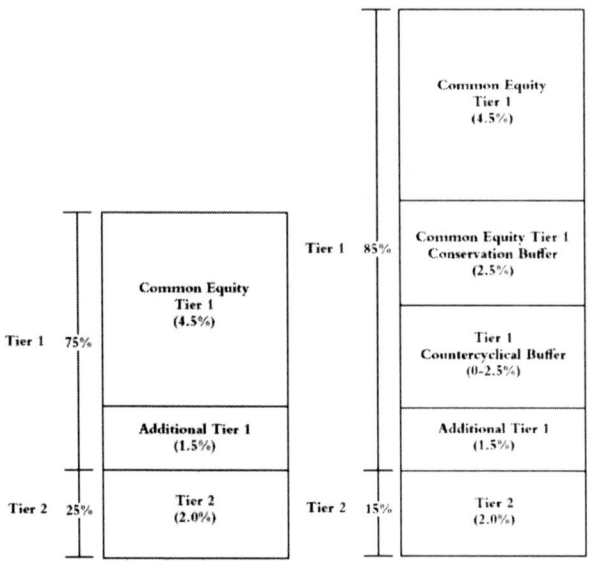

Figure 3: 8 percent Total Capital and potential 13 percent Capital Ratio [14]

3.1.1.   Tier 1 capital (excluding Buffers)

As one can see out of Figure 3, Tier 1 capital (excluding all buffers) can be divided into 2 different parts, Common Equity and Additional Tier 1 capital. Under Basel III there are very strict regulations which explain which assets account as which type of capital. Therefore, I will focus on the most important facts which assets have to fulfill. For further information one can have a look at appendix of this paper or in the new Basel 3 accord. The most important source of Common Equity capital are common stocks. Whenever a bank issues some stocks they get money from investors. But not every type of stock can be used as common equity capital. The most important factors that have to be mentioned are: [15]

---

[14] King et. Al. (2011), p.4-6
[15] Basel III (2011)

Common shares that are the most subordinated claim in the liquidation process of a bank. There is no special defined maturity of these shares. Therefore, it has a perpetual principal. When there is no liquidation process inside the bank itself, these shares cannot be paid back or cancelled out. Additionally, investors have a claim on some dividend payments but the bank is not forced to pay it. At least, there has to be some feature which allows a bank so pay dividends in profitable times. Hence, only the bank has the option to pay dividends and the investor cannot decide due to his believes. Independent of which accounting standards are used, a bank has to verify these shares as equity in their balance sheet. [16]

Beside common stock issuance a bank has also other opportunities to get some Common Equity Tier 1 capital. Firstly, they are able to get some surplus on stocks, because they were able to sell them higher than its par value. Secondly, after a bank has paid out its dividends it can use its retained earnings to increase its capital. Thirdly, a bank has to mention all the shares of subsidiary companies in the calculation of Common Equity capital. [17]

On the other side a bank has to build a 1.5% of its RWAs in form of Additional Tier 1 Capital. Also for this sort of capital, Basel III provides some regulatory rules which have to be fulfilled by banks. Again, I will focus only on the main parts but I recommend reading the Appendix to get all information from the Basel III accord. Typical assets in this section are preferred stocks which do not give the owner a voting right at the annual meeting but pay most of the time higher dividends as compensation. Contrary to common shares, it is only subordinated to some depositors and creditors of the bank. As with Common Equity capital, there is also no maturity date allowed in the regulatory rules for Additional Capital. Although, this capital class is callable but only at least five years after an investor bought it. [17]

3.1.2. Tier 2 capital

The most important point to mention for Tier 2 capital is that it gets absorbed when a bank has to declare insolvency. Therefore, the money of an issuer is not guaranteed because it gets absorb in the case of a default [17]

---

[16] Basel III (2011), p.14-15
[17] Basel III (2011)

The maturity of Tier 2 capital has to be at least 5 years. Additionally, it has to be linearly amortized during the last 5 years of the maturity. Basically, a bank has no possibility to close its position in such assets. There exist only two exceptions. Firstly, when a bank is able to issue another asset that brings as least as much money as the previous asset. The second opportunity is, when a bank can demonstrate that the sum of all other forms of Tier 2 capital is higher than the 2 percent minimum requirement. A buyer of such assets has no right to get coupon payments earlier than it is mentioned in the asset contract. The asset is allowed to give some coupon payments but it is not allowed that there are some dividend features, like common stocks have it. If the issuer of an Asset that is listed under Tier 2 capital is not directly issued by a bank, but from a special purpose vehicle (SPV), there is a need to guarantee, that all the money is available in the case of a liquidation of the bank. Again, to get in-depth knowledge it is recommended to read part C in the appendix. [18]

3.1.3.   Buffer implementation

All previous forms of capital were not new in the Basel accord. The only new thing is that there was a focus on the explanations of it. But after the financial crisis the need for an additional form of equity rose extremely. The main problem during the crisis of 2007 was the decreasing possibility of some borrowers to repay their loans. Therefore, banks had an increasing amount of losses. However, banks still paid high bonus payments to managers and also dividends to their shareholders. This strategy accelerated definitely the problems in all banks. There was no chance to recover the already quite low capital reserves. In contrast to that, they decreased even more and put more pressure on each bank and later also on the financial markets. [19]

To ensure that such problems have a lower possibility to occur, the BCBS implemented two sorts of buffers in the new Basel III accord – Conversation and Countercyclical Buffer. The main idea is that banks should save more money in economically good times, to be able to absorb potential losses in the future with this capital. When a new crisis occurs, banks should be able to maintain their daily business and be able to recover their capital much faster. [20]

---

[18] Basel III (2011)
[19] Caruana (2010)
[20] King (2011)

3.1.3.1. Conversation Buffer

Generally, the Conversation Buffer is nothing else than an additional amount of money in form of Common Equity Tier 1 Capital. The BCBS defines that banks have to hold 2.5% of this capital as a Conversation Buffer. In total, under the new Basel III accord a bank has to have 7% only in the form of Common Equity Tier 1 (2.5% Conversation Buffer + 4.5% Common Equity Tier 1 Capital). As it is mentioned in the introduction, banks have to build up this buffer in periods where they have high gains. In times where banks suffer losses this buffer should be used first, before the Common Equity Tier 1 Capital. But when this Buffer is used there are certain rules for each bank which they have to fulfill to bring it back to the defined level of 2.5%. Basically, a bank has three different possibilities to save money. (1) It can decrease its annual dividend payments. (2) It can decrease share buybacks. (3) It can decrease the bonus payments to their managers. [21]

The intentions of these rules are made because of wrong decisions which happened during the last financial crisis. However, it could be that some banks need this buffer to cover losses. Figure 4 presents the dealing of this problem by banks under Basel III. On the left side one can see the total amount of Common Equity Tier 1 Capital. As we have seen without the buffer it is 4.5%, including the buffer the sum of it is 7%. [21]

Individual bank minimum capital conservation standards

Common Equity Tier 1 Ratio	Minimum Capital Conservation Ratios (expressed as a percentage of earnings)
4.5% - 5.125%	100%
>5.125% - 5.75%	80%
>5.75% - 6.375%	60%
>6.375% - 7.0%	40%
> 7.0%	0%

Figure 4: how banks should save money when they use their conversation buffer [22]

---

[21] Basel III (2011)
[22] Basel III (2011), p.56

13

The BCBS subdivides the total Common Equity Tier 1 Ratio in 5 different categories. Depending in which category the capital of a bank is the more money it has to save in upcoming periods to recover its buffer. E.g. a banks Ratio is 5.5%. Therefore its conversation buffer is only at a level of 1% and has to recover another 1.5 percentage points. According to figure 4, a bank has to save a minimum of 80% of its upcoming earnings to do so. As already explained above, a bank can do so by reducing (1) dividend payments, (2) share buybacks or (3) bonus payments. If a bank does not want to reduce these payments, it has the opportunity to raise additional private capital. Finally, one can say that the conversation buffer is another aspect under Basel III which should make the banking business safer. [23]

3.1.3.2. Countercyclical Buffer

The financial crisis has shown how important the need of a conversation buffer is. To get a deeper knowledge why this is the case, one has to think about the following situation. Before the financial crisis interest rates were at a very low level. Therefore, banks were able to give more loans to their customers as they normally did. Especially people with no income, no assets and no job got loans (also known as NINJAs) because the default risk was quite low. Then interest rates started to increase and the default rate increased again to "normal" levels. The bubble of the extensive loan business burst. Because the housing prices went down each bank couldn't cover its losses by selling the apartments to other people. [24]

As a result, the borrowing activity shrank to very low levels. This limitation of new loan business pushed all housing prices further down and accelerated the banking problem. Banks were caught in their own trap where they couldn't get out. Some researchers argued that an ongoing borrowing business could have solved a lot of trouble in these times. The BCBS argued the same way and initialize the implementation of a conversation buffer in the capital requirements. Therefore, the countercyclical buffer can be used as an emergency pool of money. Because of this, a banks is nowadays able to maintain in the borrowing business when times getting worse. [25]

---

[23] Basel III (2011)
[24] Blackburn (2008)
[25] King (2011)

14

There is no exact number which a bank has to fulfill when they implement this buffer. The BCBS only defines a possible range between 0% and 2.5% in which the buffer should be. The real amount which the buffer should have is not directly affected by the BCBS. National authorities have the right to determine which amount of this buffer is needed. Of course, these authorities do not decide randomly when such a buffer is needed. They have to focus on some Micro- and Macro economical facts of the national economy. E.g. they have to observe the development of the gross domestic product and other economic key figures. Additionally, they need to observe the credit growth in the last months and years. On this data they have to estimate how the growth for the future will look like. If the national authorities think that a bank needs more capital for the future to maintain its loan business, they define which level of the buffer is needed. Of course, such a buffer cannot be realized after a few days of its announcement. Therefore, a bank has 12 months' time to reach the level which is defined by national authorities. Theoretically, the authorities have the right to declare some restrictions on banks that are not able to get this buffer in time. On the other hand, if the national authorities argue that the buffer is not needed anymore, a bank is able to use this capital immediately for other things. [26]

Generally, there are many different parts under the capital requirements of Basel III. Banks which have all the necessary forms of capitals should have fewer problems in future crisis. Later on, one will see in a critical analysis if this really is the case. However, the BCBS decided that RWAs should not be the only method which enables a bank and national authorities to look at its capital requirements. Hence, they implemented a leverage ratio under Basel III which is explained in the next chapter.

3.2. Leverage Ratio

Starting with the first of January 2013, each bank has to calculate its leverage ratio which presents an additional form of risk measurement system. The BCBS defined for the calculation that a bank has to compare only its Tier 1 capital with its total exposure. At the beginning of Basel III it is declared that the target leverage ratio will be at a minimum level of three percent. As a first stage, a testing period from the 1st of January 2011 until the 31th of December 2012 will show how well this target is defined. [26]

---

[26] Basel III (2011)

In Basel III it should be clear which capital can be used as Tier 1 capital and which not. Hence, the main problem, concerning the calculation of the leverage ratio, is that one has to find a correct calculation method for the exposure of default. Until now, there are several things which have to be mentioned in the calculation. It is not allowed to reduce the value of some assets, also if there are some physical or financial collateral which reduce its risk. Banks have to include the value of their derivatives. For this calculation they have to use its actual value which is declared in the balance sheet, plus an additional value to correct its future value (positively and negatively changes). However, the BCBS has the challenge to ensure every bank calculates its leverage ratio in the same way. When they will not do so, it is impossible to compare leverage ratios between different banks. Finally, one can say that the implementation of a second method which is not influenced by risk weightings extends the comparability among all banks. The BCBS expects some changes for the leverage ratio. Due to the fact that there are no experiences with such calculations, there will be some changes after a few years. At the beginning of 2017 there will be a focus on the last years and how this ratio affected banking business. In the mid of 2017 there will be an announcement of the BCBS, where they have the opportunity to make some changes according its calculation or target value. [27]

However, all the components of Basel III cannot immediately be implemented. Therefore, banks have a certain timeframe where they have to adjust to the new capital and supervisory requirements.

3.3. Step-by-Step Implementation

This chapter deals only with the implementation process of the whole Basel III accord. As it is explained in the previous chapters, such a massive change of capital requirements cannot be implemented immediately. Therefore, the BCBS decided to implement all capital ratios step-by-step. The obligatory implementation process starts with the 1st of January 2013. At the 1st of January 2019 the whole process should be finished due to the plan of the BCBS. Figure 5 gives an overview of the most important changes over the time. Until the end of 2015, almost every type of capital has to be adapted to the new Basel III rules. [27]

---

[27] Basel III (2011)

	2011	2012	2013	2014	2015	2016	2017	2018	As of 1 January 2019
Leverage Ratio	Supervisory monitoring		Parallel run 1 Jan 2013 – 1 Jan 2017 Disclosure starts 1 Jan 2015					Migration to Pillar 1	
Minimum Common Equity Capital Ratio			3.5%	4.0%	4.5%	4.5%	4.5%	4.5%	4.5%
Capital Conservation Buffer						0.625%	1.25%	1.875%	2.50%
Minimum common equity plus capital conservation buffer			3.5%	4.0%	4.5%	5.125%	5.75%	6.375%	7.0%
Phase-in of deductions from CET1 (including amounts exceeding the limit for DTAs, MSRs and financials)				20%	40%	60%	80%	100%	100%
Minimum Tier 1 Capital			4.5%	5.5%	6.0%	6.0%	6.0%	6.0%	6.0%
Minimum Total Capital			8.0%	8.0%	8.0%	8.0%	8.0%	8.0%	8.0%
Minimum Total Capital plus conservation buffer			8.0%	8.0%	8.0%	8.625%	9.25%	9.875%	10.5%
Capital instruments that no longer qualify as non-core Tier 1 capital or Tier 2 capital						Phased out over 10 year horizon beginning 2013			

Figure 5: Implementation process of Basel III [28]

[28] Basel III (2011), p.77

In the last three years, both buffers getting implemented. The quite slow implementation should ensure that banks can easily achieve the increasing capital requirements each year. Additionally, they should be able to focus on their main business without many constraints. In 2019 banks will have an 8 percent Total Capital and a 13 percent Potential Capital Ratio. [29]

4. Shortcomings

Theoretically, Basel III should make the banking business safer. But some researchers argue that there will be many shortcomings with its implementation. On the next pages, one will see main shortcomings like "shifting promises", an increase of products costs and a decrease in GDP growth.

4.1. Shifting promises

During the financial crisis one has seen an increase in ABSs and Credit Default Swaps (CDS). Due to the help of these Assets banks were able to restructure their internal risk. Under the new Basel III accord this restructuring of risk is still possible. [30] Therefore, a bank can still change its regulatory capital and its leverage ratio quite easily. The following example gives an overview how such a shift of risk can look like.

In the example bank A buys a corporate bond. To make calculations easier, assume that the bank pays 1000 USD to the company for this bond. In return, the company promises to make yearly coupon payments. By definition, the risk weighting of the company is 100 percent under Basel III. Hence, the bank has to hold 8 percent of it (80USD) in their balance sheet as capital reserve. Now, suppose that bank A is able to make a CDS on this bond with bank B and additionally, shorts the bond itself. Due to the fact that bank B has a lower risk of default, Bank A has only to hold 16 USD in their balance sheet (20 percent risk weighting * 8 percent * 1000 USD = 16). Normally, bank B has to hold the bond with 100 percent risk weighting like bank A did it before. [31]

[29] Basel III (2011)
[30] Hull (2009)
[31] Atkinson (2011)

Instead of this, bank B decides to guarantee the CDS Spread price by making a contract with an insurance company. In this example the price is set at 50 USD and the insurance company charges an additional amount of 15 USD (1.5percent of 1000USD). Such a business is identified as off balance sheet activity under Basel III and needs only a risk weighting of 50 percent. As a result, bank B has only to hold about 2.6 USD (50 percent * 8 percent * 65USD = 2.6USD. Finally, both banks were able to decrease its capital requirements from an initial value of 80USD down to 18.6 USD. This is a decrease of almost 71 percent. Without all this transaction activities, bank A would have a leverage Ratio of 12.5 percent. Due to the capital shifting, bank A increased this ratio to a new level of 53.8. Figure 6 illustrates the whole process which is explained in the example. [32]

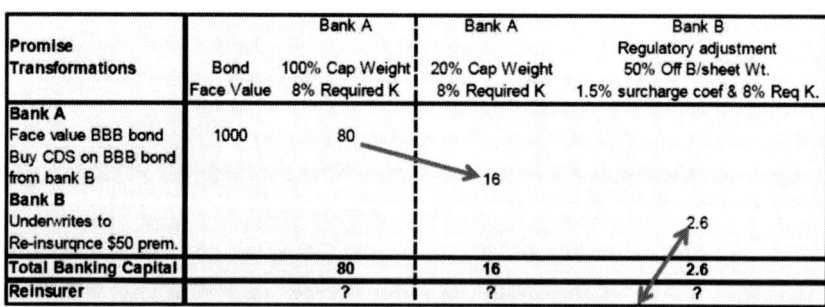

Promise Transformations	Bond Face Value	Bank A 100% Cap Weight 8% Required K	Bank A 20% Cap Weight 8% Required K	Bank B Regulatory adjustment 50% Off B/sheet Wt. 1.5% surcharge coef & 8% Req K.
Bank A Face value BBB bond Buy CDS on BBB bond from bank B	1000	80		
Bank B Underwrites to Re-insurqnce $50 prem.			16	2.6
Total Banking Capital		80	16	2.6
Reinsurer		?	?	?

Figure 6: Example of possible "shifting promises" under Basel III [33]

As one has seen with this simple example, banks are still able to shift their promises and hence, also shrink their capital requirements. Banks can easily deal with the new Basel regulations, because they avoid them by finding loopholes.

4.2. Increasing Product Costs

Due to the increasing capital requirements under Basel III, many banks will face a decreasing Return on Equity (ROE). But not every bank will be affected the same way. In a study of McKinsey, the authors tried to explain the possible changes in products costs among different banking sectors like retail or corporate banking.

---

[32] Atkinson (2010)
[33] Atkinson (2010), p.13

In previous years where banks did not have to hold such high capital requirements, they were able to use this additional money to give it to their customers in form of loans. Under Basel III a bank has to have more capital reserves depending on the business they do. Some researchers from McKinsey calculated the cost changes for different products among different sectors. The results are represented in figure 7.

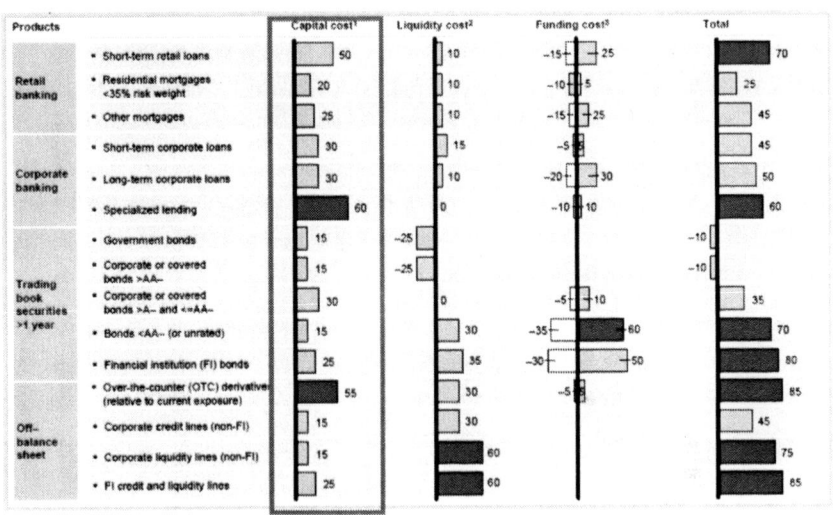

Figure 7: changing total product costs in different banking sectors [34]

The first column presents the increased costs due to changes of capital requirement. All numbers in this figure are given in Basis Points. The retail banking sector is mainly affected with increasing costs in the short-term retail loan business. This is especially affected by an increasing amount of RWA in this sector. Basically, this is needed because of a high risk potential. Generally, the probability that a retail customer cannot repay its loan increases when he has less time to do it. In contrast to that, residential mortgages with less than 35% risk weights will only lead to an increase of 20 basis points in product costs. As before, one can explain that the costs won't be that high due to a longer timeframe where the customer can payback his loan. [35]

[34] Härle (2010), p.9
[35] Härle (2010)

Generally, corporate banking business will have more problems with the new requirements. Especially Europe, which has a high concentration of small and middle-sized enterprises (SME) will suffer a lot of problems. The capital costs for specialized lending increases about 60 Basis points due to the calculation of McKinsey. Specialized lending includes especially new business projects. Basically, when a corporate tries to make a new important project it needs a certain amount of investment for it. Ex ante no one can definitely say if the project will generate a lot of profit in the future. Therefore, the risk of a bank to give loans to such projects is very high because the probability that the project will default is also quite high. Therefore, a bank which allows such loan contracts has to hold more capital reserve and will face higher capital costs. The new capital requirements do not affect off balance sheet activity of banks. These are more affected by the new liquidity requirements which are also defined under the new Basel accord. Nevertheless, Over the Counter (OTC) derivatives will face increasing product costs of 55 basis points due to higher capital requirements. [36]

One has to think about the consequences that such an increase of products costs will have to bank customers. Of course, banks want that their revenue will be the same or even better that they can increase under Basel III. Therefore, they are willing to charge more from their clients for their service. Section 4.4 explains this problem more detailed.

4.3. Decreasing GDP growth

In a last step of the shortcomings of Basel III, one will see how the implementation will force an overall decrease in worldwide GDP growth. The data is provided by a research of the OECD. The main results of it can be seen in Figure 8. The upper part of this graph shows the change in GDP level when the step-by-step implementation is at the end of 2015. As it is explained in chapter 3.3, until this point in time almost all different kinds of capital sources are implemented. Only the two types of buffers are missing. The authors of the article calculated the changes that the new capital requirements of Basel III have on the GDP growth of the three main OECD countries, USA, Japan and the Euro area. [37]

---

[36] Härle (2010)
[37] Slovik (2011)

requirements 2015	GDP level (percentages)					GDP growth (percentage points)
	Year 1	Year 2	Year 3	Year 4	Year 5	annual
United States	-0.01	-0.04	-0.07	-0.10	-0.11	-0.02
Euro area	0.00	-0.04	-0.17	-0.26	-0.39	-0.08
Japan	0.00	-0.05	-0.07	-0.17	-0.19	-0.04
Average (simple)	0.00	-0.04	-0.10	-0.17	-0.23	-0.05
Average (GDP weighted)	0.00	-0.04	-0.11	-0.17	-0.23	-0.05

requirements 2019	GDP level (percentages)					GDP growth (percentage points)
	Year 1	Year 2	Year 3	Year 4	Year 5	annual
United States	-0.05	-0.20	-0.34	-0.49	-0.59	-0.12
Euro area	0.00	-0.13	-0.51	-0.76	-1.14	-0.23
Japan	0.00	-0.12	-0.18	-0.41	-0.47	-0.09
Average (simple)	-0.02	-0.15	-0.34	-0.55	-0.73	-0.15
Average (GDP weighted)	-0.02	-0.16	-0.38	-0.58	-0.79	-0.16

Figure 8: How the changing capital requirements will change the development of GDP [38]

As one can see, the average yearly decrease for 5 years will be 0.05 percent points in comparison to a situation where Basel III is not introduced. Generally, this does not sound that dramatic but one has to remember that this calculation does not include the buffers. Therefore, the authors calculated the changes in the GDP growth when Basel III is fully introduced. In this case there will be an annually lower GDP of about 0.15 percent points. The authors explain that problem with the creation of higher product costs which will affect the whole banking business. To keep the ROE of a bank constant, the costs for customers will increase. Furthermore, the amount of loans given to clients will decrease over time. Hence, companies and private persons cannot invest in new products which will lead to a decrease of other companies' profits. The results which are presented in figure 8 also show that Europe will be the most affected part in the world when Basel III is implemented. [39]

Especially, the fact that Europe is one of the biggest losers when Basel III is implemented will bring up a lot of critics. Due to the ongoing European Crisis this implementation could accelerate the problems. But this is only one of my personal critics which are presented in the next chapter.

---

[38] Slovik (2011), p.10
[39] Slovik (2011)

4.4. Critics from a personal point of view

I totally agree with all the shortcomings that are discussed by other researchers and are explained in the previous chapters. But due to the highly cross-linked financial system there will be many more problems that will come up with the implementation of Basel III. Especially, Europe will have to deal with many more problems because the ongoing crisis is not yet solved. Additionally, all new capital requirements do not make it easier to solve it.

Generally, the European Union and especially the Euro Zone has to deal with a starting recession. Figure 9 illustrates the situation of it.

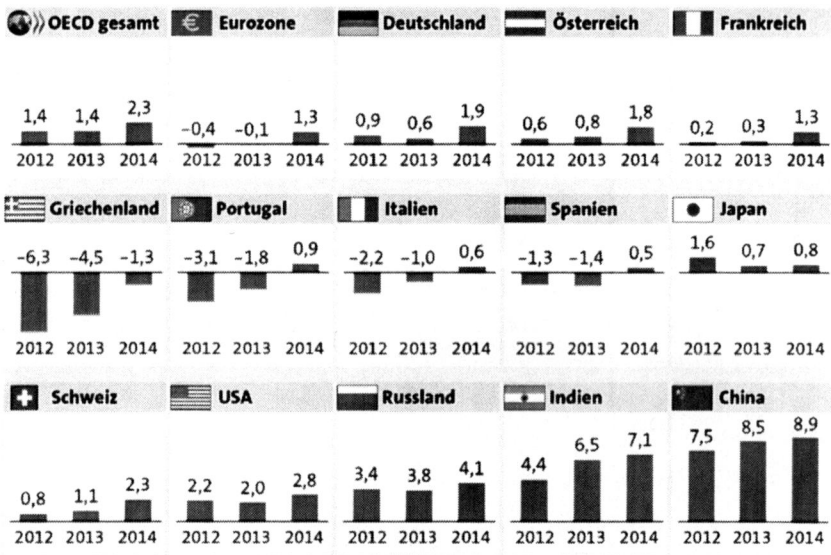

Figure 9: comparison of GDP growth between the Eurozone and other countries [40]

In the year 2012 also countries which normally had a GDP growth higher than 2 percent, like Germany or Austria, are not able to maintain these results. The countries which suffer most from the sovereign debt crisis, namely Greece, Portugal, Italy and Spain, have a decreasing GDP in 2012. Additionally, some forecasts show that all these countries will face a shrinking national economy in 2013. But one has to remember that this recession of the Eurozone happens without

---

[40] Standard (2012)

any impact from Basel III. In my opinion the introduction of Basel III is simply too early for most of the European countries. On the one hand, the European Union tries to solve the whole crisis by giving new loans to these countries, lowering interest rates etc. On the other hand, Basel III gets introduced in a few months which will make the economic recovery process even more difficult. The increase of capital requirements will lower the loan business in these countries even more. Hence, without enough loans it is quite impossible that the whole economy can grow and increase the annual GDP. Probably the recovery of these countries will last about 5-8years and not 2years like it is suggested for Portugal, Italy and Spain in figure 9.

But the implementation will not only lead to a decrease in the GDP growth. One has to think about the social changes which will happen. Basically as I have explained, the shrinking loan business leads to a shrinking economy. Therefore, some companies will have a lot of troubles to maintain in their business. In such situation a company has two possibilities to react. On the one side it can try to increase its profits, which is not possible in this case or at least not in the short run. The other possibility is to decrease its cost. The easiest way how a firm can get rid of some costs is to fire its employees. Probably, the unemployment rate of the Eurozone will get a new peak in the next few years. But like one can see e.g. in Spain also young and educated people will suffer under this problem. Another opportunity to decrease costs is to decrease the quality of the products. However, lower quality standards will drive some companies into trouble because they will get replaced by others which do not have this bad quality.

However, the banking sector will also face some upcoming problems with Basel III. The biggest problem that banks will have is the highly increasing rate of Common Equity Tier 1 capital that has to be hold. As it is explained in chapter 3.1 banks have to hold about 7 percent only as Common Equity Tier 1 capital. This type of money will be the hardest type to achieve in the next few years. The trust in the banking sector is historically on a very low point. Therefore, it will be very hard for the banks to get some capital in form of stock issues etc. Additionally, banks have higher product costs which each customer will has to pay for. This increasing cost for customers is another reason why the loan business will shrink in the next years. Like in the private sector also banks will have to decrease its costs to maintain in their business. Probably, one will see a high unemployment rate for people with a financial education background. But this seems to be the only possibility to shrink the overall Balance sheet and therefore to shrink the amount of RWAs.

Another important topic in the banking sector will be a change in the different customer groups. Due to a higher amount of capital reserves that have to be held for unsecured loans of "bad customers", banks are willing to give money to "good" ones. This change in customer segments will reduce RWAs and will lead to a small increase in the bank's profitability.

One of the most important shortcomings which have to be mentioned is a political problem of Basel III. Historically, one has seen that especially banks in the United States had problems to implement the Basel Accord or simply do not want to do so. During the Financial Crisis, where Basel II was implemented, almost no bank in the USA was able to get all requirements. Although, this was the case they had the idea to upgrade the Basel Accord in the next years. Actually, the US will not implement Basel III at this point in time. Due to the fact that the implementation is not obligatory and cannot be judged by law, the BCBS cannot really to anything to force the USA to implement Basel III. When they do not implement the new accord this has a few impacts. Firstly, the risk of the US banks will still remain high due to lower capital requirements etc. Therefore, if there will be a theoretical default, like the one of Lehman Brothers, banks all around the world will have to deal with the same problems like during the financial crisis. Although, most of the banks implement Basel III the capital will not be enough to cover all losses if one of the big banks defaults. Secondly, if the US banks do not implement Basel III they will have a competitive advantage. Customers will go to US banks because the costs for loans are smaller than in Europe where Basel III is implemented. This lower cost can be created by a lower amount of RWAs that has to be hold under Basel II.

Finally, one has to say that the shortcomings of Basel III might have an infinite end. Although, it is developed to make the banking business less risky, it will lead to the opposite effect in the short run. In my opinion the new requirements are somehow useful, but they get implemented too early. Perhaps it would be better to start the implementation in 2014 or 2015 when the overall economy has recovered itself, especially the economy of the Eurozone.

5. Conclusion

As one has seen, the implementation of capital requirements for banks is still an ongoing process. Since Basel I there were many tremendous changes in requirements or calculation for RWAs. Historically low equity ratios led to a stricter banking regulation that commits bank to have more capital reserves. Basically, the aim of the whole process is to make the banking business safer. But as one has seen during the financial crisis, the Basel accord was not well enough defined. Therefore, Basel III is a big step in the whole process of banking regulation. Generally, the total capital ratio which banks have to hold as reserves increase from 8 to 13 percent of all RWAs. Also the distribution of capital changed. Whereas, under Basel II the distribution between Tier 1 and 2 capital was 50/50, the distribution changes to 85 of Tier 1 and 15 percent Tier 2 capital. But this distribution is only true if both buffers are used fully. These two buffers are the biggest changes under Basel III. The conversation buffer is used to when banks want to pay dividends or bonuses to their managers. But they have to save money immediately to fill them back up to a level of 2.5 percent. Due to the fact that a lot of banks paid out too much dividends and bonuses during the financial crisis, this buffer should help to make these policies easier without affecting the 4.5 percent Common Equity Tier 1 capital. The countercyclical buffer can be announced by national regulators with a maximum of 2.5 percent. The aim is that banks should save money in good times to maintain especially in the loan business during bad times.

Nevertheless, the chance that the new requirements under Basel III get changed again remains due to the shortcomings which are explained in this paper. The financial crisis has shown us how dangerous shifting promises are and this problem remains under Basel III. Additionally, higher product cost for banks will lead to higher costs for customers in the loan business. The loan business will also shrink because of higher amounts of capital that has to be hold as reserves. Due to these facts, annual GDP growth will slow down when the whole Basel accord is implemented.

However, Basel III is a next important step in the history of banking regulation. Although, it is not yet perfect it has some new innovations that should make the whole financial system safer. But see in the future one will if there is another need of improvement towards a new Basel IV accord.

IV. Appendix

A. *Exact Definition of Common Equity Tier 1 Capital:* [41]

1.	Represents the most subordinated claim in liquidation of the bank.
2.	Entitled to a claim on the residual assets that is proportional with its share of issued capital, after all senior claims have been repaid in liquidation (ie has an unlimited and variable claim, not a fixed or capped claim).
3.	Principal is perpetual and never repaid outside of liquidation (setting aside discretionary repurchases or other means of effectively reducing capital in a discretionary manner that is allowable under relevant law).
4.	The bank does nothing to create an expectation at issuance that the instrument will be bought back, redeemed or cancelled nor do the statutory or contractual terms provide any feature which might give rise to such an expectation.
5.	Distributions are paid out of distributable items (retained earnings included). The level of distributions is not in any way tied or linked to the amount paid in at issuance and is not subject to a contractual cap (except to the extent that a bank is unable to pay distributions that exceed the level of distributable items).
6.	There are no circumstances under which the distributions are obligatory. Non payment is therefore not an event of default.
7.	Distributions are paid only after all legal and contractual obligations have been met and payments on more senior capital instruments have been made. This means that there are no preferential distributions, including in respect of other elements classified as the highest quality issued capital.
8.	It is the issued capital that takes the first and proportionately greatest share of any losses as they occur [13]. Within the highest quality capital, each instrument absorbs losses on a going concern basis proportionately and *pari passu* with all the others.
9.	The paid in amount is recognised as equity capital (ie not recognised as a liability) for determining balance sheet insolvency.
10.	The paid in amount is classified as equity under the relevant accounting standards.
11.	It is directly issued and paid-in and the bank can not directly or indirectly have funded the purchase of the instrument.

---

[41] Basel III (2011), p.14

26

12. The paid in amount is neither secured nor covered by a guarantee of the issuer or related entity[14] or subject to any other arrangement that legally or economically enhances the seniority of the claim.

13. It is only issued with the approval of the owners of the issuing bank, either given directly by the owners or, if permitted by applicable law, given by the Board of Directors or by other persons duly authorised by the owners.

14. It is clearly and separately disclosed on the bank's balance sheet.

B. Criteria for Additional Tier 1 Capital: [42]

1.	Issued and paid-in
2.	Subordinated to depositors, general creditors and subordinated debt of the bank
3.	Is neither secured nor covered by a guarantee of the issuer or related entity or other arrangement that legally or economically enhances the seniority of the claim vis-à-vis bank creditors
4.	Is perpetual, ie there is no maturity date and there are no step-ups or other incentives to redeem

5. May be callable at the initiative of the issuer only after a minimum of five years:

    a. To exercise a call option a bank must receive prior supervisory approval; and

    b. A bank must not do anything which creates an expectation that the call will be exercised; and

    c. Banks must not exercise a call unless:

        i. They replace the called instrument with capital of the same or better quality and the replacement of this capital is done at conditions which are sustainable for the income capacity of the bank[15]; or

        ii. The bank demonstrates that its capital position is well above the minimum capital requirements after the call option is exercised.[16]

6. Any repayment of principal (eg through repurchase or redemption) must be with prior supervisory approval and banks should not assume or create market expectations that supervisory approval will be given

7. Dividend/coupon discretion:

    a. the bank must have full discretion at all times to cancel distributions/payments[17]

    b. cancellation of discretionary payments must not be an event of default

    c. banks must have full access to cancelled payments to meet obligations as they fall due

    d. cancellation of distributions/payments must not impose restrictions on the bank except in relation to distributions to common stockholders.

8. Dividends/coupons must be paid out of distributable items

9. The instrument cannot have a credit sensitive dividend feature, that is a dividend/coupon that is reset periodically based in whole or in part on the banking organisation's credit standing.

10. The instrument cannot contribute to liabilities exceeding assets if such a balance sheet test forms part of national insolvency law.

---

[42] Basel III (2011), p.15-17

11. Instruments classified as liabilities for accounting purposes must have principal loss absorption through either (i) conversion to common shares at an objective pre-specified trigger point or (ii) a write-down mechanism which allocates losses to the instrument at a pre-specified trigger point. The write-down will have the following effects:

    a. Reduce the claim of the instrument in liquidation;

    b. Reduce the amount re-paid when a call is exercised; and

    c. Partially or fully reduce coupon/dividend payments on the instrument.

12. Neither the bank nor a related party over which the bank exercises control or significant influence can have purchased the instrument, nor can the bank directly or indirectly have funded the purchase of the instrument

13. The instrument cannot have any features that hinder recapitalisation, such as provisions that require the issuer to compensate investors if a new instrument is issued at a lower price during a specified time frame

14. If the instrument is not issued out of an operating entity or the holding company in the consolidated group (eg a special purpose vehicle – "SPV"), proceeds must be immediately available without limitation to an operating entity[18] or the holding company in the consolidated group in a form which meets or exceeds all of the other criteria for inclusion in Additional Tier 1 capital

C. *Criteria for Tier 2 capital* :[43]

1. Issued and paid-in

2. Subordinated to depositors and general creditors of the bank

3. Is neither secured nor covered by a guarantee of the issuer or related entity or other arrangement that legally or economically enhances the seniority of the claim vis-à-vis depositors and general bank creditors

4. Maturity:

    a. minimum original maturity of at least five years

    b. recognition in regulatory capital in the remaining five years before maturity will be amortised on a straight line basis

    c. there are no step-ups or other incentives to redeem

---

[43] Basel III (2011), p.26-27

5. May be callable at the initiative of the issuer only after a minimum of five years:

    a. To exercise a call option a bank must receive prior supervisory approval;

    b. A bank must not do anything that creates an expectation that the call will be exercised;[19] and

    c. Banks must not exercise a call unless:

        i. They replace the called instrument with capital of the same or better quality and the replacement of this capital is done at conditions which are sustainable for the income capacity of the bank[20]; or

        ii. The bank demonstrates that its capital position is well above the minimum capital requirements after the call option is exercised.[21]

6. The investor must have no rights to accelerate the repayment of future scheduled payments (coupon or principal), except in bankruptcy and liquidation.

7. The instrument cannot have a credit sensitive dividend feature, that is a dividend/coupon that is reset periodically based in whole or in part on the banking organisation's credit standing.

8. Neither the bank nor a related party over which the bank exercises control or significant influence can have purchased the instrument, nor can the bank directly or indirectly have funded the purchase of the instrument

9. If the instrument is not issued out of an operating entity or the holding company in the consolidated group (eg a special purpose vehicle – "SPV"), proceeds must be immediately available without limitation to an operating entity[22] or the holding company in the consolidated group in a form which meets or exceeds all of the other criteria for inclusion in Tier 2 Capital

30

V. References

Atkinson P. and Blundel-Wignal A. (2010), *Thinking beyond Basel III: Necessary Solutions for Capital and Liquidity,* OECD Journal: Financial Market Trends, p.1-23

Balin B. (2008), *Basel I, Basel II, and Emerging Markets: A Nontechnical Analysis,* John Hopkins University School of Advance International Studies

Basel I (1998), available at: http://www.bis.org/publ/bcbsc111.pdf, seen on: 01.12.2012

Basel II (2006), available at: http://www.bis.org/publ/bcbs128.pdf, seen on: 01.12.2012

Basel III (2011), available at: http://www.bis.org/publ/bcbs189.pdf, seen on: 01.12.2012

Basel Committee of Banking Supervision (BCBS), *about Basel Committee,* available at: http://www.bis.org/bcbs/ on the 01.12.2012

Berger A., Herring R. and Szegö G. (1995), *The role of capital in financial institutions,* Journal of Banking and Finance, Vol.19, p.393-430

Caruana Jame (2010), *The challenge of talking macroprudential decisions: who will press which button,* available at: http://www.bis.org/speeches/sp100928.pdf, seen on: 08.12.2012

Härle P., Lüder E., Pepanides T., Pfetsch S., Poppensieker T. and Stegemann U. (2011), *Basel III and the European banking business: Its impact, how banks might respond, and the challenges of implementation,* McKinsey working paper on risk, Vol.26 p.1-32

Hull J. (2009), *The Credit Crunch of 2007: What went wrong? Why? What lessons can be learned?,* Journal of Credit Risk, Vol.5, p.3-18

King P. and Tarbert H. (2011), *Basel III: An Overview,* Banking and Financial Policy Report, Vol.30, p.1-18

Slovik P. and Cournède B. (2011), *Macroeconomic Impact of Basel III,* OECD Department Working Papers, Nr. 844, p.1-15

Standard (2012), *OECD sieht Existenz der Eurozone bedroht,* online Ausgabe Standard from: 27.12.2012, available at: http://derstandard.at/1353207404182/OECD-sieht-Oesterreichs-Konjunktur-schwaecheln seen on: 14.12.2012

9 783656 369028